SOCIAL PROGRESS AND SUSTAINABILITY

Shelter • Safety • Literacy • Health • Freedom • Environment

AFRICA: MIDDLE, WESTERN, AND SOUTHERN

Foreword by **Michael Green,**
Executive Director, Social Progress Imperative

By Kelly Kagamas Tomkies

SOCIAL PROGRESS AND SUSTAINABILITY

SOCIAL PROGRESS AND SUSTAINABILITY

Shelter • Safety • Literacy • Health • Freedom • Environment

AFRICA: MIDDLE, WESTERN, AND SOUTHERN

Kelly Kagamas Tomkies

Foreword by
Michael Green
Executive Director, Social Progress Imperative

MASON CREST

Mason Crest
450 Parkway Drive, Suite D
Broomall, PA 19008
www.masoncrest.com

Printed and bound in the United States of America

First printing
9 8 7 6 5 4 3 2 1

Series ISBN: 978-1-4222-3490-7
Hardcover ISBN: 978-1-4222-3491-4
ebook ISBN: 978-1-4222-8386-8

Names: Tomkies, Kelly Kagamas, author.
Title: Africa : middle, western, and southern/by Kelly Kagamas Tomkies; foreword by Michael Green, executive director, Social Progress Imperative.
Other titles: Social progress and sustainability.
Description: Broomall, PA : Mason Crest, 2017. | Series: Social progress and sustainability series | Includes index.
Identifiers: LCCN 2016007602| ISBN 9781422234914 (hardback) | ISBN 9781422234907 (series) | ISBN 9781422283868 (ebook)
Subjects: LCSH: Social indicators—Africa. | Social accounting—Africa. | Africa—Social conditions—21st century.
Classification: LCC HN774 .T66 2017 | DDC 303.44096—dc23
LC record available at http://lccn.loc.gov/2016007602

Developed and Produced by Print Matters Productions, Inc. (www.printmattersinc.com)

Project Editor: David Andrews
Design: Bill Madrid, Madrid Design
Copy Editor: Laura Daly

Note on Statistics:
All social progress statistics, except where noted, are used by courtesy of the Social Progress Imperative and reflect 2015 ratings.

Contents

KEY ICONS TO LOOK FOR:

Text-Dependent Questions: These questions send readers back to the text for more careful attention to the evidence presented there.

Words to Understand: These words with their easy-to-understand definitions will increase readers' understanding of the text while building vocabulary skills.

Series Glossary of Key Terms: This back-of-the-book glossary contains terminology used throughout this series. Words found here increase readers' ability to read and comprehend higher-level books and articles in this field.

Research Projects: Readers are pointed toward areas of further inquiry connected to each chapter. Suggestions are provided for projects that encourage deeper research and analysis.

Sidebars: This boxed material within the main text allows readers to build knowledge, gain insights, explore possibilities, and broaden their perspectives by weaving together additional information to provide realistic and holistic perspectives.

FOREWORD

Michael Green
Executive Director
Social Progress Imperative

SOCIAL PROGRESS AROUND THE GLOBE

Michael Green

How do you measure the success of a country? It's not as easy as you might think.

Americans are used to thinking of their country as the best in the world, but what does "best" actually mean? For a long time, the United States performed better than any other country in terms of the sheer size of its economy, and bigger was considered better. Yet China caught up with the United States in 2014 and now has a larger overall economy.

What about average wealth? The United States does far better than China here but not as well as several countries in Europe and the Middle East.

Most of us would like to be richer, but is money really what we care about? Is wealth really how we want to measure the success of countries—or cities, neighborhoods, families, and individuals? Would you really want to be rich if it meant not having access to the World Wide Web, or suffering a painful disease, or not being safe when you walked near your home?

Using money to compare societies has a long history, including the invention in the 1930s of an economic measurement called gross domestic product (GDP). Basically, GDP for the United States "measures the output of goods and services produced by labor and property located within the U.S. during a given time period." The concept of GDP was actually created by the economist Simon Kuznets for use by the federal government. Using measures like GDP to guide national economic policies helped pull the United States out of the Great Depression and helped Europe and Japan recover after World War II. As they say in business school, if you can measure it, you can manage it.

Many positive activities contribute to GDP, such as
- Building schools and roads
- Growing crops and raising livestock
- Providing medical care

More and more experts, however, are seeing that we may need another way to measure the success of a nation.

Other kinds of activities increase a country's GDP, but are these signs that a country is moving in a positive direction?
- Building and maintaining larger prisons for more inmates
- Cleaning up after hurricanes or other natural disasters
- Buying alcohol and illegal drugs
- Maintaining ecologically unsustainable use of water, harvesting of trees, or catching of fish

GDP also does not address inequality. A few people could become extraordinarily wealthy, while the rest of a country is plunged into poverty and hunger, but this wouldn't be reflected in the GDP.

In the turbulent 1960s, Robert F. Kennedy, the attorney general of the United States and brother of President John F. Kennedy, famously said of GDP during a 1968 address to students at the University of Kansas: "It counts napalm and counts nuclear warheads and armored cars for the police to fight the riots in our cities ... [but] the gross national product does not allow for the health of our children.... [I]t measures everything in short, except that which makes life worthwhile."

For countries like the United States that already have large or strong economies, it is not clear that simply making the economy larger will improve human welfare. Developed countries struggle with issues like obesity, diabetes, crime, and environmental challenges. Increasingly, even poorer countries are struggling with these same issues.

Noting the difficulties that many countries experience as they grow wealthier (such as increased crime and obesity), people around the world have begun to wonder: What if we measure the things we really care about directly, rather than assuming that greater GDP will mean improvement in everything we care about? Is that even possible?

The good news is that it is. There is a new way to think about prosperity, one that does not depend on measuring economic activity using traditional tools like GDP.

Advocates of the "Beyond GDP" movement, people ranging from university professors to leaders of businesses, from politicians to religious leaders, are calling for more attention to directly measuring things we all care about, such as hunger, homelessness, disease, and unsafe water.

One of the new tools that have been developed is called the Social Progress Index (SPI), and it is the data from this index that is featured in this series of books, Social Progress and Sustainability.

The SPI has been created to measure and advance social progress outcomes at a fine level of detail in communities of different sizes and at different levels of wealth. This means that we can compare the performance of very different countries using one standard set of measurements, to get a sense of how well different countries perform compared to each other. The index measures how the different parts of society, including governments, businesses, not-for-profits, social entrepreneurs, universities, and colleges, work together to improve human welfare. Similarly, it does not strictly measure the actions taken in a particular place. Instead, it measures the outcomes in a place.

The SPI begins by defining what it means to be a good society, structured around three fundamental themes:
- Do people have the basic needs for survival: food, water, shelter, and safety?
- Do people have the building blocks of a better future: education, information, health, and sustainable ecosystems?

- Do people have a chance to fulfill their dreams and aspirations by having rights and freedom of choice, without discrimination, with access to the cutting edge of human knowledge?

The Social Progress Index is published each year, using the best available data for all the countries covered. You can explore the data on our website at http://socialprogressimperative.org. The data for this series of books is from our 2015 index, which covered 133 countries. Countries that do not appear in the 2015 index did not have the right data available to be included.

A few examples will help illustrate how overall Social Progress Index scores compare to measures of economic productivity (for example, GDP per capita), and also how countries can differ on specific lenses of social performance.

- The United States (6th for GDP per capita, 16th for SPI overall) ranks 6th for Shelter but 68th in Health and Wellness, because of factors such as obesity and death from heart disease.
- South Africa (62nd for GDP per capita, 63rd for SPI) ranks 44th in Access to Information and Communications but only 114th in Health and Wellness, because of factors such as relatively short life expectancy and obesity.
- India (93rd for GDP per capita, 101st for SPI) ranks 70th in Personal Rights but only 128th in Tolerance and Inclusion, because of factors such as low tolerance for different religions and low tolerance for homosexuals.
- China (66th for GDP per capita, 92nd for SPI) ranks 58th in Shelter but 84th in Water and Sanitation, because of factors such as access to piped water.
- Brazil (55th for GDP per capita, 42nd for SPI) ranks 61st in Nutrition and Basic Medical Care but only 122nd in Personal Safety, because of factors such as a high homicide rate.

The Social Progress Index focuses on outcomes. Politicians can boast that the government has spent millions on feeding the hungry; the SPI measures how well fed people really are. Businesses can boast investing money in their operations or how many hours their employees have volunteered in the community; the SPI measures actual literacy rates and access to the Internet. Legislators and administrators might focus on how much a country spends on health care; the SPI measures how long and how healthily people live. The index doesn't measure whether countries have passed laws against discrimination; it measures whether people experience discrimination. And so on.

- What if your family measured its success only by the amount of money it brought in but ignored the health and education of members of the family?
- What if a neighborhood focused only on the happiness of the majority while discriminating against one family because they were different?
- What if a country focused on building fast cars but was unable to provide clean water and air?

The Social Progress Index can also be adapted to measure human well-being in areas smaller than a whole country.

- A Social Progress Index for the Amazon region of Brazil, home to 24 million people and covering one of the world's most precious environmental assets, shows how 800 different municipalities compare. A map of that region shows where needs are greatest and is informing a development strategy for the region that balances the interests of people and the planet. Nonprofits, businesses, and governments in Brazil are now using this data to improve the lives of the people living in the Amazon region.
- The European Commission—the governmental body that manages the European Union—is using the Social Progress Index to compare the performance of multiple regions in each of 28 countries and to inform development strategies.
- We envision a future where the Social Progress Index will be used by communities of different sizes around the world to measure how well they are performing and to help guide governments, businesses, and nonprofits to make better choices about what they focus on improving, including learning lessons from other communities of similar size and wealth that may be performing better on some fronts. Even in the United States subnational social progress indexes are underway to help direct equitable growth for communities.

The Social Progress Index is intended to be used along with economic measurements such as GDP, which have been effective in guiding decisions that have lifted hundreds of millions of people out of abject poverty. But it is designed to let countries go even further, not just making economies larger but helping them devote resources to where they will improve social progress the most. The vision of my organization, the Social Progress Imperative, which created the Social Progress Index, is that in the future the Social Progress Index will be considered alongside GDP when people make decisions about how to invest money and time.

Imagine if we could measure what charities and volunteers really contribute to our societies. Imagine if businesses competed based on their whole contribution to society—not just economic, but social and environmental. Imagine if our politicians were held accountable for how much they made people's lives better, in real, tangible ways. Imagine if everyone, everywhere, woke up thinking about how their community performed on social progress and about what they could do to make it better.

Note on Text:
While Michael Green wrote the foreword and data is from the 2015 Social Progress Index, the rest of the text is not by Michael Green or the Social Progress Imperative.

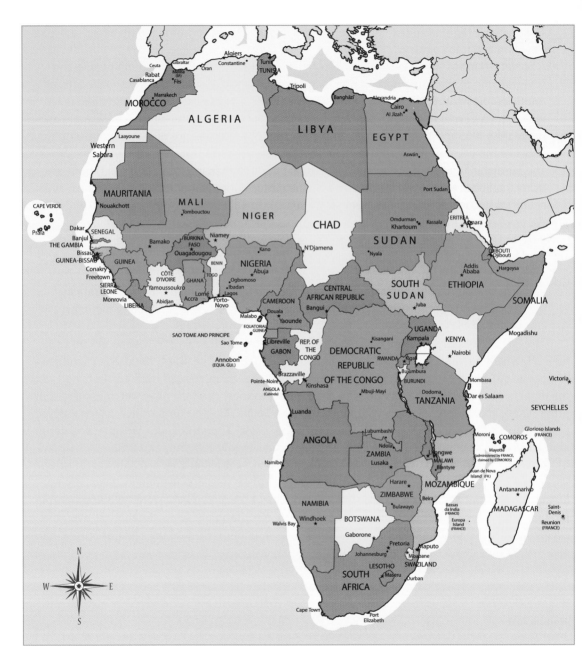

This political map shows the countries of the region discussed in this book.

SOCIAL PROGRESS IN AFRICA: MIDDLE, WESTERN, AND SOUTHERN

Of the 54 countries in Africa, those in the middle, western, and southern regions have experienced more than their share of turmoil, civil wars, corruption, and disease. Each country has a rich and interesting history that has contributed to its current social progress. For example, Liberia began as a settlement in the early 19th century for freed American slaves. These early settlers valued their hard-won freedom and independence, and within 25 years they had established a republic. It is not surprising that Liberia received one of its strongest scores from the Social Progress Imperative on the Social Progress Index (SPI) in the category of Personal Rights.

While most of these countries have a republic form of government, some have fought to convert to a constitutional democracy, while one, Lesotho, is a monarchy. In countries that have experienced civil war, many—sometimes thousands of people—have been displaced, making access to basic shelter challenging. Diseases such as AIDS and Ebola have also taken their toll on people in these regions.

However, each country continues to make progress in terms of social progress, especially in areas such as nutrition and access to medical care, which are measured by the SPI. Food security—a country's ability to provide sufficient food to meet its population's nutritional needs—is improving in many of these nations. In some, programs sponsored by UNICEF and similar governmental and nongovernmental organizations are contributing to advances in food security.

When it comes to medical care, improvements are being seen thanks to increased government spending and the development of national health care programs.

Another area where progress has been made is health and wellness, which is covered in the SPI category Foundations of Well-Being. Many of the western, middle, and southern African nations scored well in this area, as life expectancy, obesity rates, suicide rates, and the percentage of premature deaths due to indoor air pollution improved. In some countries the improvement was due to new programs in place to test, counsel, and support those with AIDs and other diseases.

The third area of social progress for these countries is tolerance/inclusion and personal rights. Although tolerance for gay and lesbian populations, as well as for some religions, is still a challenge in many countries, some, such as Angola and Gabon, have become much more inclusive. Benin and Liberia received strong scores in the area of personal rights, which means their governments do not control media outlets and what religions are practiced within their borders. In contrast, Central African Republic is considered one of the worst in the world when it comes to guaranteeing personal rights and freedoms, as you'll discover in Chapter 3.

Areas of social progress in which most of these countries need the most improvement are water, sanitation, and shelter. Since a number of them have had to put most of their resources toward defending themselves or becoming independent, they have struggled to fund the infrastructure that will ensure improved drinking water. Finding adequate shelter for thousands of people who have been displaced due to civil wars has also been a challenge in several of these countries.

Another struggle for most of these countries has been in sustaining ecosystems. In some cases, this is because of stress on the water supply. Countries such as South Africa and Swaziland have experienced severe drought conditions over the past few years. This drought, coupled with an increasing demand on water as urbanization continues to spread, has led to water shortages.

A third area in which nearly all of the countries in middle, western, and southern Africa need improvement is access to advanced education. The main reasons for their low SPI scores in this category are the lack of funding for education and the high costs of schooling. In many of these countries the cost of education is a big percentage of an average family's income, making it difficult to send children to primary schools, much less to secondary schools or universities. As regional economies improve, though, it is likely that funding for education will also improve.

A man walks along a dry ravine in the St. Phillips area of Swaziland, where drought can make life hard.

A child suffering from severe malnutrition gets screened by a volunteer in the small village of Miaki close to the town of Maradi, Niger, where food shortages are common.

CHAPTER 1

BASIC HUMAN NEEDS

Words to Understand

Communicable diseases: diseases transmitted from one person or animal to another. Also called contagious or infectious diseases.

Infrastructure: basic equipment or facilities needed for a country or area to opeate.

Mortality rate: a measure of the number of deaths over a particular period usually given per 1,000 individuals. Infant mortality rate is the death rate during the first year of life. **Child mortality rate** is the number of deaths of children less than five years old. **Maternal mortality rate** is the number of deaths due to births or pregnancy-related problems of women of reproductive age (generally defined as 15 to 44 years of age). Also called death rate.

Noncommunicable disease: a disease that is not infectious or transmitted from one person or animal to another. Examples include heart disease, stroke, and cancers.

Like many countries in Africa, the nations in the western, middle, and southern regions have histories fraught with wars, making development difficult at best. Not only did most of these countries have to fight to gain their independence from Britain, France, and other European nations, but they frequently have had to endure years of civil war. This has made building or rebuilding their economies and providing infrastructure a challenging endeavor.

Although many of these countries have ample natural resources, others depend on neighboring nations for some necessities such as food and fuel oil.

Gas flares behind a Nigerian oil worker.

For example, Botswana has exploited its abundance of diamonds to build its economy, while Nigeria has capitalized on its rich reserves of oil and natural gas. In contrast, Swaziland relies on its neighbor South Africa for 90 percent of its imports and 60 percent of its exports, due to its lack of natural resources. More details about Swaziland's imports and exports can be found in Chapter 4.

The beauty of these countries, with their plains, tropical coastlines, and mountains, along with their abundance of wildlife, makes many of them leading travel destinations, and the tourist industry has become an important and growing sector of their economies.

The SPI category Basic Human Needs covers nutrition and basic medical care, water and sanitation, shelter, and personal safety. Nearly all of the countries in these regions scored the highest on nutrition and basic medical care. Shelter, personal safety, and water and sanitation are areas that need the most improvement in order for these countries to reach the same level of social progress as more developed nations.

Basic Human Needs: Nutrition and Basic Medical Care

As in other parts of Africa, these regions are facing three major health care problems: epidemics of communicable diseases, such as HIV/AIDS and Ebola; a rise in the number of cases of noncommunicable diseases, such as heart disease; and the lack of government funding for new health care programs. Several countries are facing these challenges by focusing on preventive care, or ways to prevent diseases and other health problems as opposed to treating them.

One success story is Ghana, which in 2004 launched a national system that paid for the delivery of babies in public clinics and hospitals, missions, and private health care facilities. This system was intended to improve the maternal mortality rate and has been credited with a reduction in the maternal mortality rate of 49 percent by the end of 2013. Ghana has simultaneously increased access to contraception.

In an effort to address the quality of and access to health care, South Africa is testing a national health insurance plan that would result in health care coverage for all citizens. Currently, only about 16 percent of the population has private health insurance, with 80 percent dependent on public health care services that are badly underfunded.

Government Spending on Health Care

The World Health Organization (WHO) tracks government spending on health care as a percentage of the total. Higher percentages reflect progressive policy. Below are the percentages for selected middle, western, and southern African countries for 2011 and 2013. By comparison, the United States' percentages were 47.3 and 47.1 in 2011 and 2013, respectively, while Sweden notched 81.7 and 81.5 for those years.

Country	Public Percentage of Health Spending, 2011	Public Percentage of Health Spending, 2013
Angola	62.6	66.7
Botswana	61.6	57.1
Cameroon	34.7	34.7
Chad	43.8	36.9
Congo, Rep.	70.9	77.5
Gambia	59.8	60.1
Guinea	34.6	35.8
Mali	44.2	39.7
Mauritania	46.7	49.0
Namibia	61.8	60.4
Nigeria	31.1	27.6
South Africa	47.7	48.4

As the sidebar table shows, some countries have increased their spending, a few significantly, while others decreased their percentage of spending on health care.

Another health care statistic used by the Social Progress Imperative to measure a country's social progress is the child mortality rate. In many countries in these regions, the rate is improving. For example, in Angola, where nearly 43 percent of the country's population is under the age of 14 and the average age of its citizens is 18, the current rate is 78 per 1,000 live births. This rate was 110 in 2010, according to the World Bank.

In countries where health care spending has increased, such as the Republic of the Congo, the infant mortality rate has gone from 42 deaths in 1,000 live births in 2010 to 34 deaths in 1,000 live births by 2014. In Ghana, following the launch of its program to make deliveries of babies a free medical service to women, the infant mortality rate dropped from 50 deaths per 1,000 live births in 2010 to 44 deaths per 1,000 live births in 2014. In South Africa the rate dropped from 38 deaths per 1,000 live births in 2010 to 34 deaths per 1,000 live births in 2014.

Nutrition is another basic human need the SPI measures and for which these countries received higher scores. Since 2000 many organizations have worked together to assist countries in providing nutritious food to their populations. For example, a partnership between the European Union and UNICEF worked with Burkina Faso and Mali and two other African countries to improve food security for child survival, growth, and development. To achieve its goals, the partnership targeted one million children and 600,000 lactating and pregnant women in the four countries and promoted the use of available food and resources, breastfeeding, vitamin and mineral supplements, and other nutrition-related programs.

As a result of these and similar efforts, the food security of these nations has improved. According to the United Nations Food and Agriculture Organization, Burkina Faso's average dietary energy supply adequacy (a measure used by the UN FAO that determines whether a country's food supply can meet its population's caloric needs) in 2000 was 109 percent and increased to 123 percent by 2014. In Mali it increased from 119 to 137 percent over the same period.

A mother and her thriving child in the village of Kokemnoure, Burkina Faso, are succeeding where many struggle for food security in the country.

Basic Human Needs: Water and Shelter

Two very basic human needs are water and shelter. The Social Progress Imperative looks at several pieces of data when it comes to determining the status of a country and how it meets these two needs. As seen in the SPI, countries in middle, western, and southern Africa have much work to do in providing clean water and adequate shelter for their people. Most of these nations received their lowest scores in these subcategories.

For example, according to data provided by the WHO/UNICEF Joint Monitoring Programme for Water Safety and Sanitation, when it comes to providing improved drinking water, Angola has made little to no progress since 1990. The percentage of the country's population that had access to improved drinking water in 1990 was 45.7, and by 2015 that figure had risen to just 49 percent.

According to the United Nations Department of Economic and Social Affairs, not having access to clean drinking water relates directly to the overall health of a population. Often when there is no clean water available, residents have to drink water that is untreated and that may contain animal and human waste, resulting in disease. Children are often the most vulnerable in acquiring diseases from drinking water that hasn't been treated.

In contrast, Gambia (officially the Republic of the Gambia) met its goal of improving the supply of clean drinking water, according to the WHO/UNICEF data. By 2015 more than 90 percent of the country's population had access to clean drinking water. According to a report published by the African Ministers' Council on Water, the government of Gambia has agreed to focus on continuing improvements in water and sanitation. This is

Children near Mkuze Game Reserve, South Africa, collect water from a river with tanks and buckets.

especially important when considering that little to no progress was made on another goal by 2015, that of improving water filtration facilities. In 2006 the country adopted the National Water Resources Policy, which defined the responsibility of its Department of Water Resources in managing the resources, including licensing, data collection, analysis, and dissemination, as well as coordination at the regional, subnational, and national levels in resource management. Formalizing these responsibilities should lead to more progress in improving facilities in the future.

One reason countries in middle, western, and southern Africa scored poorly on the SPI when it comes to providing adequate shelter is the low percentages of people in these regions who have access to electricity. Without electricity in their homes, people depend on alternative fuel sources, such as burning wood, for heating and cooking, which can lead to increased indoor air pollution and sickness. In fact, according to a report published by the United Nations, exposure to smoke from traditional cook stoves and open fires, which is the primary means of cooking and heating for nearly three billion people in the developing world, including Botswana, causes 1.9 million premature deaths annually. The most affected people are women and young children. Botswana, which is located in southern Africa, has faced many challenges when it comes to meeting its energy needs. The country's demand for energy has exceeded its available resources since 2010, according to a report published by the United Nations. According to WHO, just 53 percent of the population has access to electricity. The United Nations report indicates that a leading future source of generating electricity in Botswana is expected to be solar energy.

In Senegal, which is in western Africa, 56.5 percent of the population has access to electricity; that percentage hasn't changed since 2010, according to data provided by the World Bank. Electricity availability in Côte d'Ivoire, also in western Africa, has actually declined since 2010, from 58 to 55.8 percent in 2012. Those who do have access to electricity frequently experience blackouts. According to the United Nations magazine and online site *Africa Renewal,* the leading causes of poor availability and quality of electricity in Africa are increasing demand and poorly maintained infrastructure.

Despite the low scores in the subcategories of water and shelter, it is clear that programs are in place in these regions of Africa that are expected to make a difference in the coming years.

Clean, Affordable Light

Lighting Africa, a partnership between the International Finance Corporation and the World Bank, helps African nations meet their electric energy needs. The program's goal is to help more than 250 million people gain access to clean, affordable, off-grid lighting and energy products (such as solar home systems, which aren't tied into an electric utility network system) by 2030. It is working toward achieving this goal through quality assurance, consumer education, access to financing (for businesses and product suppliers), and by working with governments to remove policy and regulatory barriers. Through products like solar systems, Lighting Africa hopes to encourage the use of sustainable and renewable energy resources, rather than traditional nonrenewable sources of energy. According to results published on the Lighting Africa website (lightingafrica.org), 35 million people have improved energy access due to modern solar lighting products.

Text-Dependent Questions

1. How does a country's government spending on health care affect the health and wellness of the people living in that country?
2. What segment of a population is most vulnerable to disease because of unclean, unsafe drinking water?
3. What is one energy alternative for people who don't have access to electricity?
4. What is one reason many people in Africa do not have access to electricity?

Research Projects

Choose one of the countries discussed in this chapter. Research green energy sources currently used there. Select one green energy source and research its potential for meeting the country's energy needs in the future.

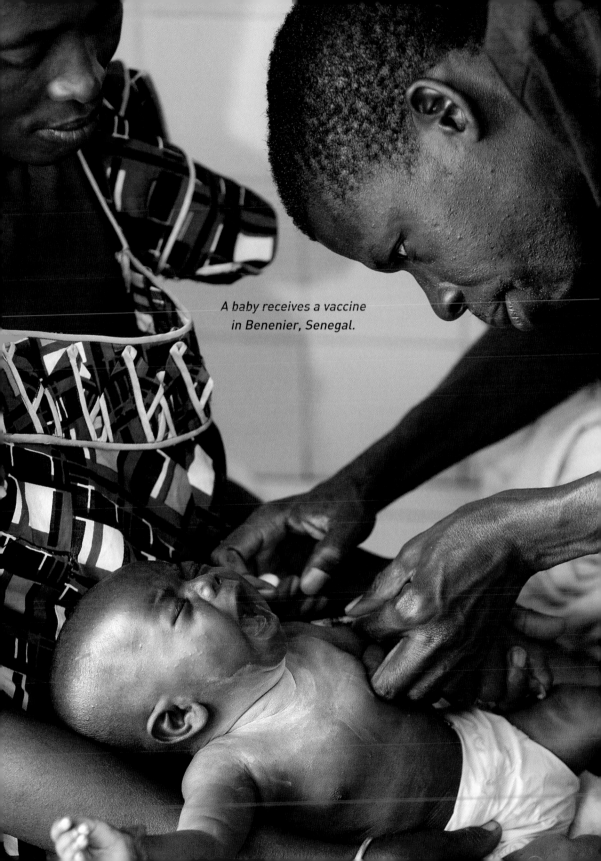

A baby receives a vaccine in Benenier, Senegal.

CHAPTER 2

FOUNDATIONS OF WELL-BEING

Words to Understand

Ecotourism: tourism to places with often threatened natural environments, especially to support conservation efforts and observe wildlife. It is considered environmentally responsible.

Greenhouse gas emissions: the release into the earth's atmosphere of gases, especially carbon dioxide, that absorb infrared radiation from the sun, which heats the air. The more of these gases that exist, the more heat is prevented from escaping into space and, consequently, the more the earth's atmosphere gets warmer. This increase in heat is known as the "greenhouse effect."

Habitat: a place where a plant, animal, or other living thing naturally or normally lives or grows.

Literacy: the ability to read and write. Computer literacy is basic, nontechnical knowledge about computers and how to use them.

Obesity: the condition of being too heavy for one's height; being too overweight.

Urbanization: the act of becoming more like cities; the process by which more and more people leave the countryside to live in towns and cities.

According to the Social Progress Imperative, there are a number of factors that determine a country's foundations of well-being: access to basic knowledge (adult literacy, primary school enrollment, etc.), access to information and communications (access to the Internet, independent newspapers and publishers, etc.), health and wellness (life expectancy, obesity rates, etc.), and ecosystem sustainability (greenhouse gas emissions, biodiversity, etc.).

Most countries in middle, western, and southern Africa scored well in the subcategory of health and wellness. There were a few notable exceptions, however. For example, Botswana had one of its lowest scores in this area, while Swaziland had one of its highest in access to basic knowledge.

As in other parts of Africa, there is still work to be done before these countries' SPI scores are comparable to those of more developed nations.

Foundations of Well-being: Health and Wellness

Many countries in middle, western, and southern Africa received high scores on the SPI in the area of health and wellness. They include Angola, the Central African Republic, Chad, Benin, Gambia, Guinea, and Togo. It is interesting to note that nine of the countries in the southern region of Africa received their highest scores in the subcategory of health and wellness.

The factors that led to the high scores are improved life expectancy, obesity rate, suicide rate, and percentage of premature deaths due to indoor air pollution.

The Democratic Republic of the Congo (also known as DR Congo) is one of the countries that received a high score. One reason for its improving health and wellness profile is the work being done in this area by Episcopal Relief and Development (ERD), an organization of the Anglican Church that has launched several initiatives in the country. For example,

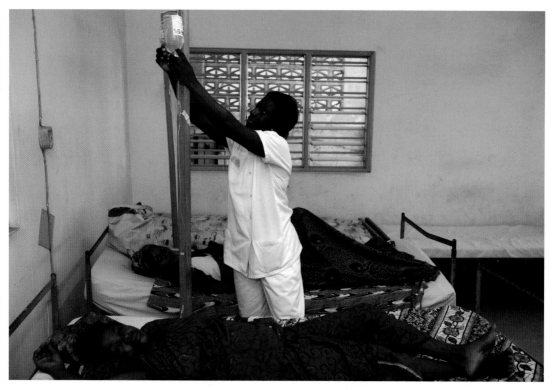

Patients with HIV and AIDS receive care at a health center in Lomé, Togo.

the ERD provides HIV/AIDS counseling, testing, treatment, and support. It also sponsors maternal and child health care and malaria treatment and prevention programs.

According to the World Bank, life expectancy in the DR Congo has slowly but steadily increased. In 2014 life expectancy was age 49; by 2014 it had increased to age 50. The number of deaths in the DR Congo from communicable diseases has also decreased. In 2000 there were 1,154 deaths per 100,000 people; by 2012 that number had decreased to 920.

One country that did not receive its highest score in this subcategory is South Africa. One factor for the Social Progress Imperative's rating is the increase in the rate of obesity there. According to a 2014 study published in the British medical journal *Lancet,* obesity is quickly becoming a leading health problem in South Africa, especially among women. The study found that 7 out of 10 women and 4 out of 10 men have significantly more body fat than what is considered healthy. In 2011 a Medical Research Council study reported that 61 percent of South Africa's population is overweight or obese. Being overweight or obese increases a person's risk of developing chronic or potentially life-threatening diseases, such as cardiovascular disease, diabetes, and chronic kidney disease.

According to the MRC study, women who live in urban areas in a higher socioeconomic category with the resources to buy more food (usually food that is unhealthy) were most at risk or inclined to become obese. The study also noted that a higher percentage of children in South Africa are becoming obese; as of 2014, 17 percent of adolescents were overweight and 4 percent obese. The study recommended preventive and interventional programs to educate those most at risk, namely young women, about the dangers of obesity.

As you can see from the table, the countries with lower obesity rates were among those that received the higher scores on the SPI in the area of health and wellness.

Obesity Rates and Rankings of Selected African Countries

This table shows the percentage of the population that is considered obese, along with that country's rank compared with the other countries in the world. For example, more than 25 percent of South Africa's population is obese, and it is the 24th most obese country in the world.

Country	Obesity Rate (%)	Rank
Angola	8.5	147
Benin	8.1	151
Botswana	19.5	128
Burkina Faso	5.2	181
Cameroon	9.6	130
Central African Republic	4.4	175
Chad	6.6	177
Congo, Dem. Rep.	3.7	185
Equatorial Guinea	16.2	129
Gambia	9.1	138
Guinea	5.9	165
Namibia	16.8	133
Niger	3.7	180
Nigeria	9.7	146
South Africa	25.6	24
Swaziland	14.8	98

Foundations of Well-being: Access to Basic Knowledge

In analyzing a country's foundations of well-being, the Social Progress Imperative considers access to basic knowledge. The factors that indicate whether this access is in place in a country include the adult literacy rate, percentage of children enrolled in primary school, mobile telephone subscriptions, percentage of the population that has access to the Internet, and freedom of the press. In

A couple on a motorbike ride past an ad for a cell phone operator in Niamey, Niger, a country that is striving to improve its citizens' access to basic knowledge.

middle, western, and southern Africa, SPI scores for access to basic knowledge were either high or low. Some countries received their highest scores in this area, while others received their lowest.

Countries that received their highest SPI scores in access to basic knowledge were Cameroon, Republic of the Congo, Cape Verde, Ghana, Botswana, Lesotho, Namibia, South Africa, and Swaziland. The Central African Republic, Chad, Burkina Faso, Guinea, Liberia, Mauritania, Niger, Nigeria, and Senegal all received their lowest scores in this area.

One reason Cameroon received a high score is because of government efforts to increase the number of children enrolled in primary school. According to the United Nations Educational, Scientific and Cultural Organization (UNESCO), there were approximately 2.77 million children enrolled in primary school in 2000. By 2014 that number had increased to more than 4.1 million. One program in Cameroon is taking literacy a step further, by endeavoring to improve computer literacy in the country. The DUNGRI-Computer Center Project designed by the Computer Department of the NAVTI Foundation (navtifoundation.org) is working to create community computer centers in schools and villages in Cameroon.

Ghana has also made great strides in improving its adult literacy rate, increasing the number of adults ages 15 to 24 who are literate from 70.66 percent in 2000 to an estimated 90.6 percent in 2015. The country is also partnering with the US government to launch a program to increase literacy rates for children. The United States Agency for International Development (USAID) is collaborating with the Ghana Ministry of Education and the Ghana Education Service in its program called Partnership for Education: Learning.

Students attend class in an outdoors elementary school classroom in the Yilo Krobo District near Accra in eastern Ghana.

The goal is to reach more than two million children in Ghana to improve early-grade literacy.

In several countries in middle, western, and southern Africa adult literacy rates are very low or not measured. In Chad the percentage of the population ages 15 to 24 that is considered literate was estimated to be just 50 percent in 2015. In Niger this percentage was just 26 percent, and in Senegal it was 56 percent. Although these percentages are low compared to other African countries, it is important to note that they are improvements from previous years' figures. For example, in Chad the adult literacy rate was just 37 percent in 2000. In Niger the rate was 19 percent in 2001, and in Senegal it was 49.2 in 2001. So these percentages are improving at a healthy rate.

One project launched and completed in Niger in 2011 by the Center for Global Development was a mobile telephone education program. The program taught participants how to use their mobile phones as a way of improving reading and math skills.

Primary school enrollment was also low for these lower-scoring countries, according to data provided by UNESCO. For example, in the Central African Republic in 2012, the most recent year data is available, 72 percent of children were enrolled in primary school. In Burkina Faso just 68 percent were enrolled as of 2013. The country with the lowest primary school enrollment percentage is Liberia, with just 38 percent of children enrolled. This is mainly due to the country's prolonged civil war, which prevented advancements in education as well as other social progress efforts. USAID, the lead US government agency working to reduce poverty in developing nations, is hoping to increase the opportunities for both boys and girls to attend school.

Foundations of Well-being: Ecosystem Sustainability

The SPI measures three main factors—greenhouse gas emissions, water withdrawals as a percentage of resources (water usage as a percentage of water available), and biodiversity and habitat protection—in assessing ecosystem sustainability. The countries in middle, western, and southern Africa with the lowest SPI scores in this category were Angola, Cameroon, the DR Congo, Benin, Cape Verde, Gambia, Ghana, Mali, Lesotho, Namibia, South Africa, and Swaziland. One country in this region, Burkina Faso, received its highest score in this category.

One reason South Africa received a low score in this area is that it is experiencing very high stress on water resources, according to the World Resources Institute. Urbanization rates have increased in the country (nearly 65 percent of South Africans now live in cities), which creates an increased demand on water. In addition, climate change has reduced rainfall, which has significantly reduced water reserves. Because of the expanding population and growing economy, access to clean water and sanitation has become more challenging for many people in the nation.

Swaziland is another country experiencing high stress on its water supply, according to The Water Project (thewaterproject.org), a nonprofit organization that works with local groups and communities to provide clean, safe water. The Water Project estimates that 40 percent of the country's residents do not have access to clean water. Nonfunctioning infrastructure is one of the reasons for this stress.

Burkina Faso has made significant improvements to its water supply, primarily through collaborations with other nations to fund water and sanitation projects. The country's commitment to improving both urban and rural water supplies and treatment systems has led to its high scores in this area.

Tourists observe elephants in the Chobe National Park, northern Botswana.

The Yale Center for Environmental Law and Policy and the Columbia University Center for International Earth Science Network publish a yearly Environmental Performance Index (epi.yale.edu), which ranks countries on their efforts to protect biodiversity and wildlife habitat. Botswana has been recognized by the index for its efforts.

Biodiversity and Wildlife Protection

Here is how some selected countries in the middle, western, and southern regions of Africa ranked in the area of biodiversity and wildlife protection, according to the Environmental Performance Index (EPI).

Country	EPI Rank
Botswana	1
Namibia	19
Guinea-Bissau	32
Senegal	39
Burkina Faso	42
Gabon	45
Côte d'Ivoire	47
Niger	56
Benin	80
South Africa	84
Nigeria	100

One reason for Botswana's success is the government's plan made official in February 2007 to maintain the country's biodiversity and protect its wildlife and natural areas. This focus confirms the growing importance of tourism, including ecotourism, to Botswana's economy.

Text-Dependent Questions

1. What has led to South Africa's low SPI score for health and wellness?
2. What is one reason Cameroon has improved its SPI score in the area of access to basic knowledge?
3. Why are some southern African countries experiencing stress on their supplies of water?
4. What is one reason Botswana works hard to maintain biodiversity?

Research Projects

Research how civil war in Liberia has had an impact on the education of its children and adults.

Mourners of all race_
respect at the pass_
Nelson Mandela outsi_
home near Johannes_
South Africa. Man_
resistance to the oppre_
regime of white South _
succeeded in establi_
political rights for p_
of color and advancing_
material n_

CHAPTER 3

OPPORTUNITY

Words to Understand

Nongovernmental organization (NGO): a nonprofit, voluntary citizens' group organized on a local, national, or international level. Examples include organizations that support human rights, advocate for political participation, and work for improved health care.

Primary education: generally, basic education for children (usually ages 5 to 11), including reading, writing, and basic math. For most countries, primary education is mandatory. Also called elementary education.

Public sector: the part of a country's economy that includes the basic services provided by the government, such as infrastructure (bridges, roads, tunnels, telecommunications, sewers, water and electricity supply, etc.), military, police, public transportation, and public education and health care. The private sector is the part of the economy run by individuals and companies for profit.

Secondary education: generally, education past the primary level. In developed countries, it is usually mandatory.

Tertiary education: third-level or postsecondary education; generally, college degree programs. Includes universities, community colleges, nursing schools, research laboratories, and other institutions that offer academic degrees, certificates, or diplomas.

O pportunity is a category of the Social Progress Index that encompasses several factors. Generally, it refers to the freedoms that people in a country are able to enjoy, such as political rights, freedom of speech, freedom

Opportunity: Tolerance and Inclusion

The SPI looks at several measurements to determine the status of a country's progress when it comes to tolerating and including all people within its borders. It considers how much a government tolerates immigrants, gay and lesbian populations, minorities, and all religious groups. Countries in middle and

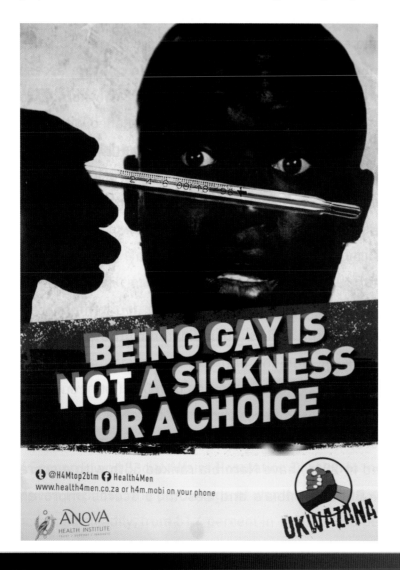

An awareness poster in Zimbabwe promotes tolerance through understanding in one of the most antihomosexual countries in the world.

western Africa with high SPI scores in this area are Angola, Cameroon, Chad, Republic of the Congo, Democratic Republic of the Congo, Gabon, Guinea, Mauritania, Niger, and Sierra Leone.

Angola, for example, shows much greater tolerance for gay and lesbian residents. There are openly gay performers, and one soap opera broadcast in the country features openly gay characters. In Gabon same-sex relationships are not criminalized, which is not the case in other African countries. However, according to a 2014 report published by the nonprofit group Human Rights First (humanrightsfirst.org), continuing discrimination against gays and lesbians has been reported there.

To determine the level of religious tolerance, the SPI uses the Pew Research Center Government Restrictions Index (pewforum.org/2014/01/14/appendix-2-government-restrictions-index), which looks at a country's efforts to restrict or prohibit the practice of a particular religion, as well as whether a government gives preferential treatment to a religion. Côte d'Ivoire, Nigeria, Togo, Botswana, Lesotho, Namibia, and Swaziland were considered particularly tolerant.

One country that had been considered a model of religious tolerance, the Central African Republic, has in recent years become a scene of bloody fighting between mostly Muslim rebel forces and Christian, or anti-balaka, militias supporting the government. Reports of massacres of Muslim civilians and other atrocities committed by the anti-balaka militias, along with forced conversion to Christianity, prompted the deployment of UN, African Union, and French armed forces to try to stabilize the country and prevent further civilian deaths. A ceasefire was signed in July 2014, but in December 2015 a separate republic was declared by rebel leaders.

Opportunity: Personal Rights

Personal rights as measured by the SPI include political rights, freedom of speech, freedom of assembly, and freedom of movement. Countries in middle, western, and southern Africa that received high scores in this area were Benin, Burkina Faso, Ghana, Liberia, Mali, Senegal, and South Africa.

People are busy with daily activities: meetings, talks, trade, and transportation on a main street and marketplace in Gbarnga in Liberia.

The SPI uses information published by Freedom House (freedomhouse. org), a US-based nongovernmental organization that reports on the status of political freedom and human rights in 195 countries.

According to Freedom House, one of the countries it calls "the worst of the worst" when it comes to political freedom is the Central African Republic because of the political instability, violence, and religious cleansing, along with the displacement of more than one million people in the conflict between rebel forces and militias.

Benin, one of the countries that received a high score in the area of personal rights, has earned a status of "free" from Freedom House. On a scale of 1 to 7, with 1 being the best and 7 being the worst, Benin received a freedom rating of 2, and also received a 2 for civil liberties and political rights. Although these are good scores, Freedom House notes that the country did experience some political unrest, with an attempted coup of the government in 2012 and 2013. In May 2014 the country's president pardoned those participating in the coup.

In examining freedom of speech, assembly, and movement, the SPI relies on data provided by the CIRI Human Rights Dataset (humanrightsdata.com). The project, which examined the human rights records of 202 countries between 1981 and 2011, gave countries whose governments did not censor people's speech a score of 2. If the government censored some people's speech, the country received a score of 1. If it completely censored all speech, the country got a score of 0.

Burkina Faso received a score of 2 for personal speech, which meant there was no government censorship or ownership of broadcast or print media outlets in the country. It earned either 2s or 1s for the other areas of freedom examined by the SPI. Ghana and Senegal received 1s (some ownership or censorship of media exists) for freedom of speech and mostly 2s for the other freedoms.

Senegalese celebrate the smooth transition of power on the streets of Dakar after a presidential run-off election that was heralded as a victory for democracy in Africa when the incumbent accepted defeat and congratulated the winner.

Opportunity: Access to Advanced Education

Nearly every country in this volume received its lowest SPI scores in the area of access to advanced education. Advanced education is learning that takes place beyond the primary education, or elementary school, level, usually at the secondary and tertiary education, or college, level.

When determining the status of a country's access to advanced education, the SPI examines several factors: the average number of years of tertiary training people age 25 or older receive, the average number of years of school attended by women between the ages of 25 and 34, and the degree of inequality in the amount of education attained among its citizens.

Tertiary Education in Middle, Western, and Southern African Countries

This table shows the percentage of the population (over the age of 25) that completed tertiary training or education in these nations (as of 2010).

Country	Percentage Tertiary
Benin	1.96
Botswana	2.79
Cameroon	1.55
Central African Republic	1.23
Congo, Rep.	1.32
Côte d'Ivoire	3.91
Congo, Dem. Rep.	1.08

Country	Percentage Tertiary
Gabon	7.88
Gambia	1.21
Ghana	2.14
Lesotho	0.77
Liberia	5.26
Mali	1.22
Mauritania	1.45
Namibia	1.42
Niger	0.70
Senegal	2.28
Sierra Leone	0.91
South Africa	0.60
Swaziland	3.27
Togo	1.79

As the sidebar table indicates, rates of completion of tertiary education are very low in most countries, with Gabon and Liberia having the highest percentages and South Africa and Niger having the lowest. One reason for South Africa's low rate may be the fact that education at all levels in the country, including the university level, is expensive and continuing to increase, according to statistics published by the South African government. The cost of tuition through the university level has risen 53 percent since 2010.

The good news is that there is not a high degree of inequality between men and women when it comes to higher education. For example, in Botswana, women age 25 or older completed 8.7 years of education, while men of the same age completed 9.0, according to data published by the World Bank. The same holds true in South Africa, where women age 25 and older completed 9.8 years of schooling, while men of the same age completed 10.1.

Text-Dependent Questions

1. Why is birth control an important focus in Côte d'Ivoire?
2. Why does Freedom House consider the Central African Republic one of the "worst of the worst" when it comes to political freedom?
3. What is one reason most of the middle, western, and southern African nations received their lowest scores on the SPI in the category of access to advanced education?

Research Projects

Research the history of violence between the Christian anti-balaka militias and the Muslim rebels in the Central African Republic.

Ships dock in the port of Luderitz, Namibia, a town popular for its diamond mining.

CHAPTER 4

MIDDLE, WESTERN, AND SOUTHERN AFRICAN COUNTRIES AT A GLANCE

ANGOLA

QUICK STATS
Population: 19,625,353
Urban Population: 44% of total population
Comparative Size: slightly less than twice the size of Texas
Gross Domestic Product (per capita): $7,200 (141st worldwide)
Gross Domestic Product (by sector): agriculture 10.2%, industry 61.4%, services 28.4%
Government: republic; multiparty presidential regime
Languages: Portuguese (official), Bantu and other African languages

SOCIAL PROGRESS SNAPSHOT
Social Progress Index: 40.00 (–21.00 below 61 world average)
Basic Human Needs: 41.27 (–27.06 below 68.33 world average)
Foundations of Well-being: 52.20 (–14.25 below 66.45 world average)
Opportunity: 26.51 (–21.72 below 48.23 world average)

Angola is still rebuilding since the end of its 27-year civil war in 2002. Its economy is overwhelmingly driven by its oil sector. Oil production and its supporting activities contribute about 50% of GDP, more than 70% of government revenue, and more than 90% of the country's exports. Diamonds contribute an additional 5% to exports. Subsistence agriculture provides the main livelihood for most of the people, but half of the country's food is still imported.

Luanda, Angola, is both the national capital and the nation's chief seaport.

ow the index every year at socialprogressimperative.org.
:k Stats from CIA World Factbook.

MIDDLE, WESTERN, AND SOUTHERN AFRICAN COUNTRIES AT A GLANCE **53**

Village de Guede Codji, Benin—a group of people is standing at a well. One man is pumping, the children are drinking the water. The well is providing clean water for the village.

BENIN

QUICK STATS

Population: 10,448,647
Urban Population: 44% of total population
Comparative Size: slightly smaller than Pennsylvania
Gross Domestic Product (per capita): $1,900 (205th worldwide)
Gross Domestic Product (by sector): agriculture 31.8%, industry 12.3%, services 55.9%
Government: republic
Languages: French (official), Fon and Yoruba (most common vernaculars in south), tribal languages (at least six major ones in north)

SOCIAL PROGRESS SNAPSHOT

Social Progress Index: 50.04 (–10.96 below 61 world average)
Basic Human Needs: 50.41 (–17.92 below 68.33 world average)
Foundations of Well-being: 58.96 (–7.49 below 66.45 world average)
Opportunity: 40.73 (–7.50 below 48.23 world average)

Present-day Benin was the site of Dahomey, a West African kingdom that rose to prominence in about 1600 and over the next two and a half centuries became a regional power, largely based on its slave trade. A move to representative government began in 1989. Two years later, free elections ushered in former Prime Minister Nicephore Soglo as president, marking the first successful transfer of power in Africa from a dictatorship to a democracy.

BOTSWANA

QUICK STATS

Population: 2,182,719
Urban Population: 57.4% of total population
Comparative Size: slightly smaller than Texas
Gross Domestic Product (per capita): $16,000 (99th worldwide)
Gross Domestic Product (by sector): agriculture 1.9%, industry 28.7%, services 69.4%
Government: parliamentary republic
Languages: Setswana 78.2%, Kalanga 7.9%, Sekgalagadi 2.8%, English (official) 2.1%, Sesarwa 1.9%, Sempukushu 1.7%, other 5.1%, unspecified 0.2% (2001 est.)

SOCIAL PROGRESS SNAPSHOT

Social Progress Index: 65.22 (+4.22 above 61 world average)
Basic Human Needs: 65.51 (–2.82 below 68.33 world average)
Foundations of Well-being: 71.69 (+5.24 above 66.45 world average)
Opportunity: 58.46 (+10.23 above 48.23 world average)

Formerly the British protectorate of Bechuanaland, Botswana adopted its new name at independence in 1966. More than four decades of uninterrupted civilian leadership, progressive social policies, and significant capital investment have created one of the most stable economies in Africa. Botswana has one of the world's highest known rates of HIV/AIDS infection, but it also has one of Africa's most progressive and comprehensive programs for dealing with the disease.

BURKINA FASO

QUICK STATS

Population: 18,931,686
Urban Population: 29.9% of total population
Comparative Size: slightly larger than Colorado
Gross Domestic Product (per capita): $1,700 (212th worldwide)
Gross Domestic Product (by sector): agriculture 38.0%, industry 22.0%, services 40.0%
Government: parliamentary republic
Languages: French (official), native African languages belonging to Sudanic family spoken by 90% of the population

SOCIAL PROGRESS SNAPSHOT

Social Progress Index: 48.82 (–12.18 below 61 world average)
Basic Human Needs: 46.56 (–21.77 below 68.33 world average)
Foundations of Well-being: 57.79 (–8.66 below 66.45 world average)
Opportunity: 42.11 (–6.12 below 48.23 world average)

Burkina Faso (formerly Upper Volta) achieved independence from France in 1960. Its high population growth and limited natural resources result in poor economic prospects for the majority of its citizens. A new three-year program of the International Monetary Fund was approved in 2013 to focus on improving the quality of public investment and ensuring inclusive growth. Political insecurity in neighboring Mali, unreliable energy supplies, and poor transportation links pose long-term challenges.

With more than 3 million inhabitants, Douala, Cameroon, is the largest city in Cameroon and its commercial capital.

CAMEROON

QUICK STATS

Population: 23,739,218
Urban Population: 54.4% of total population
Comparative Size: slightly larger than California
Gross Domestic Product (per capita): $3,000 (189th worldwide)
Gross Domestic Product (by sector): agriculture 19.9%, industry 27.6%, services 52.5%
Government: republic; multiparty presidential regime
Languages: 24 major African language groups, English (official), French (official)

SOCIAL PROGRESS SNAPSHOT

Social Progress Index: 47.42 (−13.58 below 61 world average)
Basic Human Needs: 48.48 (−19.85 below 68.33 world average)
Foundations of Well-being: 58.15 (−8.30 below 66.45 world average)
Opportunity: 35.61 (−12.62 below 48.23 world average)

French Cameroon became independent in 1960 as the Republic of Cameroon. The country has generally enjoyed stability, which has enabled the development of agriculture, roads, and railways, as well as an oil industry. Despite slow movement toward democratic reform, political power remains firmly in the hands of President Paul Biya, who has been president since 1982. Oil remains Cameroon's main export commodity, accounting for nearly 40% of export earnings despite falling global oil prices.

CAPE VERDE

QUICK STATS

Population: 545,993
Urban Population: 65.5% of total population
Comparative Size: slightly larger than Rhode Island
Gross Domestic Product (per capita): $6,300 (157th worldwide)
Gross Domestic Product (by sector): agriculture 10.0%, industry 18.6%, services 71.4%
Government: republic
Languages: Portuguese (official), Crioulo (a blend of Portuguese and West African words)

SOCIAL PROGRESS SNAPSHOT

Foundations of Well-being: 70.50 (+4.05 above 66.45 world average)
(Not all scores computed due to data gaps in statistical sources.)

The uninhabited islands were discovered and colonized by the Portuguese in the 15th century. Cape Verde's expatriate population is greater than its domestic one. Most Cape Verdeans have both African and Portuguese ancestors. The island economy suffers from a poor natural resource base, including serious water shortages, exacerbated by cycles of long-term drought, and poor soil for growing food on several of the islands, requiring it to import most of what it consumes.

CENTRAL AFRICAN REPUBLIC

QUICK STATS

Population: 5,391,539
Urban Population: 40.0% of population
Comparative Size: slightly smaller than Texas
Gross Domestic Product (per capita): $600 (230th worldwide)
Gross Domestic Product (by sector): agriculture 55.1%, industry 12.5%, services 32.3%
Government: republic
Languages: French (official), Sangho (national language), tribal languages

SOCIAL PROGRESS SNAPSHOT

Social Progress Index: 31.42 (-29.58 below 61 world average)
Basic Human Needs: 26.81 (-41.52 below 68.33 world average)
Foundations of Well-being: 44.84 (-21.61 below 66.45 world average)
Opportunity: 22.62 (-25.61 below 48.23 world average)

The former French colony of Ubangi-Shari became the Central African Republic upon independence in 1960. After three tumultuous decades of misrule—mostly by military governments—civilian rule was established in 1993 but lasted only a decade. Subsistence agriculture, together with forestry and mining, remains the backbone of the economy of the Central African Republic, with about 60% of the population living in outlying areas. The agricultural sector generates more than half of GDP. The country has been seriously destabilized by the conflict between rebel forces and government-backed militias.

Two women cook a lunch that will be served with bread to family in Moundou, Chad. Kitchen conditions lag modernity.

CHAD

QUICK STATS

Population: 11,631,456
Urban Population: 22.5% of total population
Comparative Size: slightly more than three times the size of California
Gross Domestic Product (per capita): $2,600 (194th worldwide)
Gross Domestic Product (by sector): agriculture 54.3%, industry 13.2%, services 32.4%
Government: republic
Languages: French (official), Arabic (official), Sara (in south), more than 120 different languages and dialects

SOCIAL PROGRESS SNAPSHOT

Social Progress Index: 33.17 (–27.83 below 61 world average)
Basic Human Needs: 28.09 (–40.24 below 68.33 world average)
Foundations of Well-being: 44.12 (–22.33 below 66.45 world average)
Opportunity: 27.30 (–20.93 below 48.23 world average)

Chad, part of France's African holdings until 1960, endured three decades of civil war, as well as invasions by Libya, before peace was restored in 1990. The government eventually drafted a democratic constitution and held flawed presidential elections in 1996 and 2001. Chad's landlocked location results in high transportation costs for imported goods and dependence on neighboring countries. Oil and agriculture are mainstays of Chad's economy.

CONGO, DEMOCRATIC REPUBLIC OF THE

QUICK STATS
Population: 79,375,136
Urban Population: 42.5% of total population
Comparative Size: slightly less than one-fourth the size of US
Gross Domestic Product (per capita): $700 (228th worldwide)
Gross Domestic Product (by sector): agriculture 40.4%, industry 23.0%, services 36.6%
Government: republic
Languages: French (official), Lingala (common language in business), Kingwana (a dialect of Kiswahili or Swahili), Kikongo, Tshiluba

SOCIAL PROGRESS SNAPSHOT
Foundations of Well-being: 47.69 (–18.76 below 66.45 world average)
Opportunity: 26.26 (–21.97 below 48.23 world average)
(Not all scores computed due to data gaps in statistical sources.)

Established as an official Belgian colony in 1908, the then-Republic of the Congo gained its independence in 1960, but its early years were marred by political and social instability. The economy of the Democratic Republic of the Congo—a nation endowed with vast natural resources—is slowly recovering after decades of decline. Systemic corruption since independence in 1960, combined with countrywide instability and conflict that began in the mid-1990s, has dramatically reduced national output and government revenue.

CONGO, REPUBLIC OF THE

QUICK STATS
Population: 4,755,097
Urban Population: 65.4% of total population
Comparative Size: slightly smaller than Montana
Gross Domestic Product (per capita): $6,600 (156th worldwide)
Gross Domestic Product (by sector): agriculture 3.3%, industry 74.4%, services 22.3%
Government: republic
Languages: French (official), Lingala and Monokutuba (lingua franca trade languages), many local languages and dialects (of which Kikongo is the most widespread)

SOCIAL PROGRESS SNAPSHOT
Social Progress Index: 49.60 (–11.40 below 61 world average)
Basic Human Needs: 40.67 (–27.66 below 68.33 world average)
Foundations of Well-being: 66.56 (+0.11 above 66.45 world average)
Opportunity: 41.58 (–6.65 below 48.23 world average)

Upon independence in 1960, the former French region of Middle Congo became the Republic of the Congo. A quarter century of experimentation with Marxism was abandoned in 1990, and a democratically elected government took office in 1992. The economy is a mixture of subsistence farming and hunting, an industrial sector based largely on oil, and government spending.

CÔTE D'IVOIRE

QUICK STATS

Population: 23,295,302
Urban Population: 54.2% of total population
Comparative Size: slightly larger than New Mexico
Gross Domestic Product (per capita): $3,100 (191st worldwide)
Gross Domestic Product (by sector): agriculture 25.9%, industry 21.9%, services 52.1%
Government: republic; multiparty presidential regime established 1960
Languages: French (official), 60 native dialects of which Dioula is the most widely spoken

SOCIAL PROGRESS SNAPSHOT

Basic Human Needs: 47.09 (–21.24 below 68.33 world average)
Opportunity: 31.58 (–16.65 below 48.23 world average)
(Not all scores computed due to data gaps in statistical sources.)

Close ties to France following independence in 1960, the development of cocoa production for export, and foreign investment all made Côte d'Ivoire one of the most prosperous of the West African states but did not protect it from political turmoil. Côte d'Ivoire is heavily dependent on agriculture and related activities, which engage roughly two-thirds of the population. Côte d'Ivoire is the world's largest producer and exporter of cocoa beans and a significant producer and exporter of coffee and palm oil.

GABON

QUICK STATS

Population: 1,705,336
Urban Population: 87.2% of total population
Comparative Size: slightly smaller than Colorado
Gross Domestic Product (per capita): $22,900 (79th worldwide)
Gross Domestic Product (by sector): agriculture 3.7%, industry 61.7%, services 34.6%
Government: republic; multiparty presidential regime
Languages: French (official), Fang, Myene, Nzebi, Bapounou/Eschira, Bandjabi

SOCIAL PROGRESS SNAPSHOT

Basic Human Needs: 61.91 (–6.42 below 68.33 world average)
Opportunity: 48.07 (–0.16 below 48.23 world average)
(Not all scores computed due to data gaps in statistical sources.)

El Hadj Omar Bongo Ondimba, one of the longest-serving heads of state in the world, dominated the country's political scene for four decades (1967–2009) following independence from France in 1960. Gabon's small population, abundant natural resources, and considerable foreign support have helped make it one of the more stable African countries.

Gambian women collect water from a well for their vegetable plots.

GAMBIA

QUICK STATS

Population: 1,967,709
Urban Population: 59.6% of total population
Comparative Size: slightly less than twice the size of Delaware
Gross Domestic Product (per capita): $1,600 (210th worldwide)
Gross Domestic Product (by sector): agriculture 22.8%, industry 11.8%, services 65.5%
Government: republic
Languages: English (official), Mandinka, Wolof, Fula, other indigenous languages

SOCIAL PROGRESS SNAPSHOT

Basic Human Needs: 57.90 (–10.43 below 68.33 world average)
Foundations of Well-being: 55.36 (–11.09 below 66.45 world average)
(Not all scores computed due to data gaps in statistical sources.)

Gambia (also called the Gambia) gained its independence from the UK in 1965. It relies heavily on tourism and remittances from workers overseas (accounting for about 20% of GDP). The government has invested strongly in the agriculture sector because three-quarters of the population depends on agriculture for its livelihood. In December 2015 President Yahya Jammeh, who first gained power following a military coup in 1994 and has remained in power since, declared Gambia an Islamic state, the Islamic Republic of the Gambia. Tension between Gambia and Senegal, its neighbor and former partner in a federation in the 1980s, remains.

The town and the creek are busy with shoppers on market day in Elmina, Ghana. Visible at right is Fort Coenraadsburg, a UNESCO World Heritage Site.

GHANA

QUICK STATS

Population: 26,327,649
Urban Population: 54% of total population
Comparative Size: slightly smaller than Oregon
Gross Domestic Product (per capita): $4,100 (176th worldwide)
Gross Domestic Product (by sector): agriculture 22.0%, industry 14.4%, services 40.9%
Government: constitutional democracy
Languages: English (official), Asante 16%, Ewe 14%, Fante 11.6%, Boron (Brong) 4.9%, Dagomba 4.4%, Dangme 4.2%, Dagarte (Dagaba) 3.9%, Kokomba 3.5%, Akyem 3.2%, Ga 3.1%, other 31.2%

SOCIAL PROGRESS SNAPSHOT

Social Progress Index: 58.29 (–2.71 below 61 world average)
Basic Human Needs: 55.50 (–12.83 below 68.33 world average)
Foundations of Well-being: 68.43 (+1.98 above 66.45 world average)
Opportunity: 50.93 (+2.70 above 48.23 world average)

Formed from the merger of the British colony of the Gold Coast and the Togoland trust territory, Ghana in 1957 became the first sub-Saharan country in colonial Africa to gain its independence. Ghana's economy was strengthened by a quarter century of relatively sound management, a competitive business environment, and sustained reductions in poverty levels, but in recent years it has suffered the consequences of loose fiscal policy, high budget and current account deficits, and a depreciating currency.

GUINEA

QUICK STATS

Population: 11,780,162
Urban Population: 37.2% of total population
Comparative Size: slightly smaller than Oregon
Gross Domestic Product (per capita): $1,300 (220th worldwide)
Gross Domestic Product (by sector): agriculture 20.2%, industry 44.5%, services 35.3%
Government: republic
Languages: French (official)

SOCIAL PROGRESS SNAPSHOT

Social Progress Index: 39.60 (–21.40 below 61 world average)
Basic Human Needs: 40.00 (–28.33 below 68.33 world average)
Foundations of Well-being: 51.20 (–15.25 below 66.45 world average)
Opportunity: 27.59 (–20.64 below 48.23 world average)

Guinea is at a turning point after decades of authoritarian rule since gaining its independence from France in 1958. The first free and competitive democratic presidential and legislative elections were held in 2010 and 2013, respectively, but political unrest continues. Opposition leader Mamadou Oury Bah returned to Guinea in January 2016 from exile following a pardon over charges related to a 2011 attempt on President Alpha Condé's life. Condé was elected to a second term in 2015. The Ebola epidemic of 2014–2015 affected the population, but the country was declared Ebola free in December 2015. Malnutrition, HIV/AIDS, and malaria are prevalent. Guinea has the world's largest reserves of bauxite and untapped high-grade iron ore reserves (Simandou), as well as gold and diamonds.

GUINEA-BISSAU

QUICK STATS

Population: 1,726,170
Urban Population: 49.3% of total population
Comparative Size: slightly less than three times the size of Connecticut
Gross Domestic Product (per capita): $1,400 (219th worldwide)
Gross Domestic Product (by sector): agriculture 45.0%, industry 7.5%, services 47.5%
Government: republic
Languages: Crioulo 90.4%, Portuguese 27.1% (official), French 5.1%, English 2.9%, other 2.4%

SOCIAL PROGRESS SNAPSHOT

(Scores not computed due to data gaps in statistical sources.)

Since independence from Portugal in 1974, Guinea-Bissau has experienced considerable political and military upheaval. Following mediation by the Economic Community of Western African States, a civilian transitional government assumed power in 2012 and remained until José Mário Vaz won free and fair elections in 2014. Guinea-Bissau is highly dependent on subsistence agriculture, cashew nut exports, and foreign assistance. The legal economy is based on farming and fishing, but illegal logging and trafficking in narcotics are also important economic activities.

A man stands with his bicycle in a crowd in Gabú in rural Guinea-Bissau.

Villagers show their farming tools in Roma, Lesotho.

LESOTHO

QUICK STATS

Population: 1,947,701
Urban Population: 27.3% of total population
Comparative Size: slightly smaller than Maryland
Gross Domestic Product (per capita): $2,800 (192nd worldwide)
Gross Domestic Product (by sector): agriculture 7.5%, industry and services 14.0% (most of the population is engaged in subsistence agriculture)
Government: parliamentary constitutional monarchy
Languages: Sesotho (official, southern Sotho), English (official), Zulu, Xhosa

SOCIAL PROGRESS SNAPSHOT

Social Progress Index: 52.27 (-8.73 below 61 world average)
Basic Human Needs: 48.62 (-19.71 below 68.33 world average)
Foundations of Well-being: 55.82 (-10.63 below 66.45 world average)
Opportunity: 52.35 (+4.12 above 48.23 world average)

Basutoland was renamed the Kingdom of Lesotho upon independence from the UK in 1966. The Basuto National Party ruled the country during its first two decades. Small, mountainous, and completely landlocked by South Africa, Lesotho depends on a narrow economic base of textiles manufacturing and agriculture. About three-fourths of the people live in rural areas and engage in animal herding and subsistence agriculture, although Lesotho produces less than 20% of the nation's demand for food. About 40% of the population lives below the international poverty line, and the prevalence of HIV/AIDS is estimated to be 23.6%.

A Liberian woman smiles as she leaves a doctor's room after getting treatment for her sick child at a clinic in Grand Kru County, Liberia.

LIBERIA

QUICK STATS

Population: 4,195,666
Urban Population: 49.7% of total population
Comparative Size: slightly larger than Tennessee
Gross Domestic Product (per capita): $900 (225th worldwide)
Gross Domestic Product (by sector): agriculture 38.8%, industry 16.4%, services 44.7%
Government: republic
Languages: English 20%, official; some 20 ethnic group languages, few of which can be written or used in correspondence

SOCIAL PROGRESS SNAPSHOT

Social Progress Index: 44.89 (–16.11 below 61 world average)
Basic Human Needs: 41.15 (–27.18 below 68.33 world average)
Foundations of Well-being: 53.23 (–13.22 below 66.45 world average)
Opportunity: 40.30 (–7.93 below 48.23 world average)

Settlement of freed slaves from the US in what is today Liberia began in 1822; by 1847 the new settlers were able to establish a republic. Military rule, political unrest, and civil wars in the 1980s and 1990s led to the deaths and displacement of an estimated 500,000 people and devastated the Liberian economy. A peace agreement was reached in 2003, and open elections were held in 2005. About 85 percent of the population lives below the international poverty line, and the country relies heavily on foreign assistance. It is richly endowed with water, mineral resources, forests, and a climate favorable to agriculture. Its principal exports are iron ore, rubber, gold, and timber.

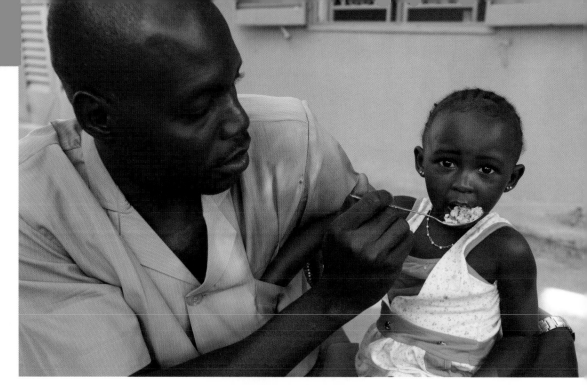

A girl enjoys breakfast with her father in Bamako, Mali.

MALI

QUICK STATS

Population: 16,955,536
Urban Population: 39.9% of total population
Comparative Size: slightly less than twice the size of Texas
Gross Domestic Product (per capita): $1,700 (215th worldwide)
Gross Domestic Product (by sector): agriculture 38.0%, industry 23.3%, services 38.7%
Government: republic
Languages: French (official), Bambara 46.3%, Peul/Foulfoulbe 9.4%, Dogon 7.2%, Maraka/Soninke 6.4%, Malinke 5.6%, Sonrhai/Djerma 5.6%, Minianka 4.3%, Tamacheq 3.5%, Senoufo 2.6%, unspecified 0.6%, other 8.5% (Note: Mali has 13 national languages in addition to its official language.)

SOCIAL PROGRESS SNAPSHOT

Social Progress Index: 46.51 (−14.49 below 61 world average)
Basic Human Needs: 48.48 (−19.85 below 68.33 world average)
Foundations of Well-being: 52.45 (−14.00 below 66.45 world average)
Opportunity: 38.60 (−9.63 below 48.23 world average)

The Sudanese Republic and Senegal became independent of France in 1960 as the Mali Federation. When Senegal withdrew after only a few months, what formerly made up the Sudanese Republic was renamed Mali. Rule by dictatorship was brought to a close in 1991 by a military coup that ushered in a period of democratic rule. In 2012 Tuareg rebels gained control of Azawad, the northern part of the country, and declared secession. Islamist rebels also gained territory, and in 2013 French military forces aided the Malian army in retaking the area. Among the 25 poorest countries in the world, Mali depends on gold mining and agricultural exports for revenue.

MAURITANIA

QUICK STATS

Population: 3,596,702
Urban Population: 59.9% of total population
Comparative Size: slightly larger than three times the size of New Mexico
Gross Domestic Product (per capita): $4,300 (182nd worldwide)
Gross Domestic Product (by sector): agriculture 48.7%, industry 16.6%, services 34.2%
Government: presidential republic
Languages: Arabic (official and national), Pulaar, Soninke, Wolof (all national languages), French

SOCIAL PROGRESS SNAPSHOT

Social Progress Index: 45.85 (–15.15 below 61 world average)
Basic Human Needs: 47.73 (–20.60 below 68.33 world average)
Foundations of Well-being: 59.08 (–7.37 below 66.45 world average)
Opportunity: 30.73 (–17.50 below 48.23 world average)

Gaining independence from France in 1960, Mauritania annexed the southern third of the former Spanish Sahara (now Western Sahara) in 1976 but relinquished it after three years of raids by the Polisario guerrilla front seeking independence for the territory. The nation's coastal waters are among the richest fishing areas in the world, and fishing accounts for about 25% of government budget revenues, but overexploitation threatens this key source of income.

NAMIBIA

QUICK STATS

Population: 2,212,307
Urban Population: 46.7% of total population
Comparative Size: slightly more than half the size of Alaska
Gross Domestic Product (per capita): $10,800 (128th worldwide)
Gross Domestic Product (by sector): agriculture 6.2%, industry 30.0%, services 63.7%
Government: republic
Languages: Oshiwambo languages 48.9%, Nama/Damara 11.3%, Afrikaans 10.4% (common language of most of the population and about 60% of the white population), Otjiherero languages 8.6%, Kavango languages 8.5%, Caprivi languages 4.8%, English (official) 3.4%, other African languages 2.3%, other 1.7%

SOCIAL PROGRESS SNAPSHOT

Social Progress Index: 62.71 (+1.71 above 61 world average)
Basic Human Needs: 59.73 (–8.60 below 68.33 world average)
Foundations of Well-being: 71.93 (+5.48 above 66.45 world average)
Opportunity: 56.47 (+8.24 above 48.23 world average)

Namibia has been governed by the Marxist South West Africa People's Organization (SWAPO) since the country won independence in 1990, although the party has dropped much of its Marxist ideology. Marine diamond mining is becoming increasingly important as the terrestrial diamond supply has dwindled. Namibia is the world's fifth-largest producer of uranium. It also produces large quantities of zinc and is a smaller producer of gold and copper.

A health care worker in Niger vaccinates children against meningitis.

NIGER

QUICK STATS

Population: 18,045,729
Urban Population: 18.7% of total population
Comparative Size: slightly less than twice the size of Texas
Gross Domestic Product (per capita): $1,000 (223rd worldwide)
Gross Domestic Product (by sector): agriculture 37.7%, industry 18.6%, services 43.7%
Government: republic
Languages: French (official), Hausa, Djerma

SOCIAL PROGRESS SNAPSHOT

Social Progress Index: 40.56 (–20.44 below 61 world average)
Basic Human Needs: 40.55 (–27.78 below 68.33 world average)
Foundations of Well-being: 48.99 (–17.46 below 66.45 world average)
Opportunity: 32.15 (–16.08 below 48.23 world average)

Niger became independent from France in 1960. Since independence it has experienced three periods of military rule and established five constitutions. After a military coup in 2010, Niger became a democratic, multiparty state. A landlocked, sub-Saharan nation, Niger's economy centers on subsistence crops, livestock, and some of the world's largest uranium deposits. Agriculture contributes nearly 40% of GDP and provides a livelihood for most of the population. Niger consistently ranks as one of the lowest on the United Nations Human Development Index.

A general view of businesses in the downtown Ikeja district, Lagos, Nigeria, Africa's most populous nation, which depends on oil for 70 percent of its tax revenue.

NIGERIA

QUICK STATS

Population: 181,562,056
Urban Population: 47.8% of total population
Comparative Size: about six times the size of Georgia; slightly more than twice the size of California
Gross Domestic Product (per capita): $6,000 (159th worldwide)
Gross Domestic Product (by sector): agriculture 20.6%, industry 25.6%, services 53.8%
Government: federal republic
Languages: English (official), Hausa, Yoruba, Igbo (Ibo), Fulani, over 500 additional indigenous languages

SOCIAL PROGRESS SNAPSHOT

Social Progress Index: 43.31 (–17.69 below 61 world average)
Basic Human Needs: 39.04 (–29.29 below 68.33 world average)
Foundations of Well-being: 61.51 (–4.94 below 66.45 world average)
Opportunity: 29.37 (–18.86 below 48.23 world average)

British influence and control over what would become Nigeria, Africa's most populous country, grew through the 19th century. A series of constitutions after World War II granted Nigeria greater autonomy; independence came in 1960. Following an April 2014 statistical "rebasing" exercise, Nigeria has emerged as Africa's largest economy, with 2014 GDP estimated at $479 billion. Oil has been a dominant source of government revenues since the 1970s. It is considered an emerging market by the World Bank and a regional power in Africa.

SENEGAL

QUICK STATS

Population: 13,975,834
Urban Population: 43.7% of total population
Comparative Size: slightly smaller than South Dakota
Gross Domestic Product (per capita): $2,500 (196th worldwide)
Gross Domestic Product (by sector): agriculture 17.1%, industry 24.3%, services 58.6%
Government: republic
Languages: French (official), Wolof, Pulaar, Jola, Mandinka

SOCIAL PROGRESS SNAPSHOT

Social Progress Index: 56.46 (–4.54 below 61 world average)
Basic Human Needs: 60.35 (–7.98 below 68.33 world average)
Foundations of Well-being: 65.97 (–0.48 below 66.45 world average)
Opportunity: 43.07 (–5.16 below 48.23 world average)

Senegal remains one of the most stable democracies in Africa and has a long history of participating in international peacekeeping and regional mediation. Senegal's economy is driven by mining, construction, tourism, fisheries, and agriculture, which is the primary source of employment in rural areas. The country's key export industries include phosphate mining, fertilizer production, agricultural products, and commercial fishing, and it is also working on oil exploration projects.

SIERRA LEONE

QUICK STATS

Population: 5,879,098
Urban Population: 39.9% of total population
Comparative Size: slightly smaller than South Carolina
Gross Domestic Product (per capita): $2,000 (200th worldwide)
Gross Domestic Product (by sector): agriculture 66.8%, industry 3.4%, services 29.8%
Government: constitutional democracy
Languages: English (official, regular use limited to literate minority), Mende (main language in the south), Temne (main language in the north), Krio (English-based Creole, spoken by the descendants of freed Jamaican slaves who were settled in the Freetown area, a first language for 10% of the population but understood by 95%)

Makeshift checkpoints were part of Sierra Leone's fight against the Ebola virus.

SOCIAL PROGRESS SNAPSHOT

Basic Human Needs: 34.43 (–33.90 below 68.33 world average)
Opportunity: 36.16 (–12.07 below 48.23 world average)
(Not all scores computed due to data gaps in statistical sources.)

Democracy is slowly being reestablished in Sierra Leone after the civil war (1991–2002) that resulted in tens of thousands of deaths and the displacement of more than two million people (about one-third of the population). Sierra Leone is extremely poor, and nearly half of the working-age population engages in subsistence agriculture.

Young girls play in an open field near King William's Town, South Africa.

SOUTH AFRICA

QUICK STATS

Population: 53,675,563
Urban Population: 64.8% of total population
Comparative Size: slightly less than twice the size of Texas
Gross Domestic Product (per capita): $13,000 (115th worldwide)
Gross Domestic Product (by sector): agriculture 2.4%, industry 18.0%, services 66.0%
Government: republic
Languages: IsiZulu (official) 22.7%, IsiXhosa (official) 16%, Afrikaans (official) 13.5%, English (official) 9.6%, Sepedi (official) 9.1%, Setswana (official) 8%, Sesotho (official) 7.6%, Xitsonga (official) 4.5%, siSwati (official) 2.5%, Tshivenda (official) 2.4%, isiNdebele (official) 2.1%, sign language 0.5%, other 1.6% (2011 est.)

SOCIAL PROGRESS SNAPSHOT

Social Progress Index: 65.64 (+4.64 above 61 world average)
Basic Human Needs: 64.59 (–3.74 below 68.33 world average)
Foundations of Well-being: 69.94 (+3.49 above 66.45 world average)
Opportunity: 62.38 (+14.15 above 48.23 world average)

South Africa is a middle-income, emerging market with an abundant supply of natural resources; well-developed financial, legal, communications, energy, and transport sectors; and a stock exchange that is Africa's largest and among the top 20 in the world. Even though the country's modern infrastructure supports a relatively efficient distribution of goods to major urban centers throughout the region, unstable electricity supplies retard growth. Economic growth has decelerated in recent years, slowing to just 1.5% in 2014.

King Mswati III watches the Umhlanga ceremony in Ludzidzini, Swaziland. The traditional Umhlanga, or Reed Dance, in which thousands of young women dance for the Queen Mother and King Mswati III, is the cultural highlight of the year in Swaziland.

SWAZILAND

QUICK STATS
Population: 1,435,613
Urban Population: 21.3% of total population
Comparative Size: slightly smaller than New Jersey
Gross Domestic Product (per capita): $7,800 (147th worldwide)
Gross Domestic Product (by sector): agriculture 7.2%, industry 47.4%, services 45.4%
Government: monarchy
Languages: English (official, used for government business), siSwati (or Swazi, official)

SOCIAL PROGRESS SNAPSHOT
Social Progress Index: 50.94 (–10.06 below 61 world average)
Basic Human Needs: 53.34 (–14.99 below 68.33 world average)
Foundations of Well-being: 57.02 (–9.43 below 66.45 world average)
Opportunity: 42.45 (–5.78 below 48.23 world average)

A constitution came into effect in 2006, but the legal status of political parties was not defined, and it remains unclear. Swaziland has surpassed Botswana as having the world's highest-known HIV/AIDS prevalence rate. Swaziland depends heavily on South Africa for more than 90% of its imports and 60% of its exports. Swaziland's currency is pegged to the South African rand, effectively relinquishing Swaziland's monetary policy to South Africa.

A mother puts charcoal on a stove in Togo.

TOGO

QUICK STATS

Population: 7,552,318
Urban Population: 40% of total population
Comparative Size: slightly smaller than West Virginia
Gross Domestic Product (per capita): $1,400 (216th worldwide)
Gross Domestic Product (by sector): agriculture 27.6%, industry 33.9%, services, 38.5%
Government: republic under transition to multiparty democratic rule
Languages: French (official, language of commerce), Ewe and Mina (main languages in the south), Kabye (sometimes spelled Kabiye) and Dagomba (main languages in the north)

SOCIAL PROGRESS SNAPSHOT

Social Progress Index: 46.66 (–14.34 below 61 world average)
Basic Human Needs: 45.11 (–23.22 below 68.33 world average)
Foundations of Well-being: 59.40 (–7.05 below 66.45 world average)
Opportunity: 35.46 (–12.77 below 48.23 world average)

French Togoland became the Republic of Togo in 1960. Democratic gains since 2005 allowed Togo to hold its first relatively free and fair legislative elections in October 2007. After years of political unrest and condemnation from international organizations for human rights abuses, Togo is finally being welcomed into the international community. This small sub-Saharan economy depends heavily on both commercial and subsistence agriculture, which provides employment for a significant share of the labor force.

Conclusion

There are few countries in the world that have experienced the turbulent and violent histories that the middle, western, and southern regions of Africa have. Whether fighting for their independence against foreign occupation or fighting within their borders for independence from dictator-style leadership, these countries have had little time and resources to spend improving social conditions. If they are not battling physical wars, they may be struggling to overcome corruption and disease. Each country has a varied, rich history that has led to its current social progress. These countries' governments and economies have contributed a great deal to their social progress. While change in many areas has been slow in coming, that doesn't mean progress isn't being made. Despite civil wars that have led to millions of displaced people, and the difficulty in gathering the monetary and human resources needed to build infrastructure for transportation, water treatment facilities, and schools, many of these countries have initiated programs that are changing things such as health care and the availability of primary and higher education.

With help from neighboring countries, the United Nations, and other nongovernmental organizations, many of the countries in these regions of Africa are working together to meet their citizens' basic needs, from improved drinking water, to alternative sources of electricity such as solar power.

Other improvements, such as in nutrition, access to medical care, and food security, are also being seen in most of the countries in these regions. While more progress still needs to be made, it is clear steps are being taken toward further social progress.

Series Glossary

Anemia: a condition in which the blood doesn't have enough healthy red blood cells, most often caused by not having enough iron

Aquifer: an underground layer of water-bearing permeable rock, from which groundwater can be extracted using a water well

Asylum: protection granted by a nation to someone who has left their native country as a political refugee

Basic human needs: the things people need to stay alive: clean water, sanitation, food, shelter, basic medical care, safety

Biodiversity: the variety of life that is absolutely essential to the health of different ecosystems

Carbon dioxide (CO_2): a greenhouse gas that contributes to global warming and climate change

Censorship: the practice of officially examining books, movies, and other media and art, and suppressing unacceptable parts

Child mortality rate: the number of children that die before their fifth birthday for every 1,000 babies born alive

Communicable diseases: medical conditions spread by airborne viruses or bacteria or through bodily fluids such as malaria, tuberculosis, and HIV/AIDS; also called **infectious diseases**; differ from **noncommunicable diseases**, medical conditions not caused by infection and requiring long-term treatment such as diabetes or heart disease

Contraception: any form of birth control used to prevent pregnancy

Corruption: the dishonest behavior by people in positions of power for their own benefit

Deforestation: the clearing of trees, transforming a forest into cleared land

Desalination: a process that removes minerals (including salt) from ocean water

Discrimination: the unjust or prejudicial treatment of different categories of people, especially on the grounds of race, age, or sex

Ecosystem: a biological community of interacting organisms and their physical environment

Ecosystem sustainability: when we care for resources like clean air, water, plants, and animals so that they will be available to future generations

Emissions: the production and discharge of something, especially gas or radiation

Ethnicities: social groups that have a common national or cultural tradition

Extremism: the holding of extreme political or religious views; fanaticism

Famine: a widespread scarcity of food that results in malnutrition and starvation on a large scale

Food desert: a neighborhood or community with no walking access to affordable, nutritious food

Food security: having enough to eat at all times

Greenhouse gas emissions: any of the atmospheric gases that contribute to the greenhouse effect by absorbing infrared radiation produced by solar warming of the earth's surface. They include carbon dioxide (CO_2), methane (CH_4), nitrous oxide (NO_2), and water vapor.

Gross domestic product (GDP): the total value of all products and services created in a country during a year

GDP per capita (per person): the gross domestic product divided by the number of people in the country. For example, if the GDP for a country is one hundred million dollars ($100,000,000) and the population is one million people (1,000,000), then the GDP per capita (value created per person) is $100.

Habitat: environment for a plant or animal, including climate, food, water, and shelter

Incarceration: the condition of being imprisoned

Income inequality: when the wealth of a country is spread very unevenly among the population

Indigenous people: culturally distinct groups with long-standing ties to the land in a specific area

Inflation: when the same amount money buys less from one day to the next. Just because things cost more does not mean that people have more money. Low-income people trapped in a high inflation economy can quickly find themselves unable to purchase even the basics like food.

Infrastructure: permanent features required for an economy to operate such as transportation routes and electric grids; also systems such as education and courts

Latrine: a communal outdoor toilet, such as a trench dug in the ground

Literate: able to read and write

Malnutrition: lack of proper nutrition, caused by not having enough to eat, not eating enough of the right things, or being unable to use the food that one does eat

Maternal mortality rate: the number of pregnant women who die for every 100,000 births.

Natural resources: industrial materials and assets provided by nature such as metal deposits, timber, and water

Nongovernmental organization (NGO): a nonprofit, voluntary citizens' group organized on a local, national, or international level. Examples include organizations that support human rights, advocate for political participation, and work for improved health care.

Parliament: a group of people who are responsible for making the laws in some kinds of government

Prejudice: an opinion that isn't based on facts or reason

Preventive care: health care that helps an individual avoid illness

Primary school: includes grades 1–6 (also known as elementary school); precedes **secondary** and **tertiary education**, schooling beyond the primary grades; secondary generally corresponds to high school, and tertiary generally means college-level

Privatization: the transfer of ownership, property, or business from the government to the private sector (the part of the national economy that is not under direct government control)

Sanitation: conditions relating to public health, especially the provision of clean drinking water and adequate sewage disposal

Stereotypes: are common beliefs about the nature of the members of a specific group that are based on limited experience or incorrect information

Subsistence agriculture: a system of farming that supplies the needs of the farm family without generating any surplus for sale

Surface water: the water found above ground in streams, lakes, and rivers

Tolerance: a fair, objective, and permissive attitude toward those whose opinions, beliefs, practices, racial or ethnic origins, and so on differ from one's own

Trafficking: dealing or trading in something illegal

Transparency: means that the government operates in a way that is visible to and understood by the public

Universal health care: a system in which every person in a country has access to doctors and hospitals

Urbanization: the process by which towns and cities are formed and become larger as more and more people begin living and working in central areas

Well-being: the feeling people have when they are healthy, comfortable, and happy

Whistleblower: someone who reveals private information about the illegal activities of a person or organization

Index

RESOURCES

Continue exploring the world of development through this assortment of online and print resources. Follow links, stay organized, and maintain a critical perspective. Also, seek out news sources from outside the country in which you live.

Websites

Social Progress Imperative: socialprogressimperative.org
United Nations—Human Development Indicators: hdr.undp.org/en/countries and Sustainable Development Goals: un.org/sustainabledevelopment/sustainable-development-goals
World Bank—World Development Indicators: data.worldbank.org/data-catalog/world-development-indicators
World Health Organization—country statistics: who.int/gho/countries/en
U.S. State Department—human rights tracking site: humanrights.gov/dyn/countries.html
Oxfam International: oxfam.org/en
Amnesty International: amnesty.org/en
Human Rights Watch: hrw.org
Reporters without Borders: en.rsf.org
CIA—The World Factbook: cia.gov/library/publications/the-world-factbook

Books

Literary and classics

The Good Earth, Pearl S. Buck
Grapes of Wrath, John Steinbeck
The Jungle, Upton Sinclair

Nonfiction—historical/classic

Angela's Ashes, Frank McCourt
Lakota Woman, Mary Crow Dog with Richard Erdoes
Orientalism, Edward Said
Silent Spring, Rachel Carson
The Souls of Black Folk, W.E.B. Du Bois

Nonfiction: development and policy—presenting a range of views

Behind the Beautiful Forevers: Life, Death, and Hope in a Mumbai Undercity, Katherine Boo
The Bottom Billion: Why the Poorest Countries Are Failing and What Can Be Done About It, Paul Collier
The End of Poverty, Jeffrey D. Sachs
For the Common Good: Redirecting the Economy toward Community, the Environment, and a Sustainable Future, Herman E. Daly
I Am Malala: The Girl Who Stood Up for Education and Was Shot by the Taliban, Malala Yousafzai and Christina Lamb
The Life You Can Save: Acting Now to End World Poverty, Peter Singer
Mismeasuring Our Lives: Why GDP Doesn't Add Up, Joseph E. Stiglitz, Amartya Sen, and Jean-Paul Fitoussi
Rachel and Her Children: Homeless Families in America, Jonathan Kozol
The White Man's Burden: Why the West's Efforts to Aid the Rest Have Done So Much Ill and So Little Good, William Easterly

Foreword writer Michael Green is an economist, author, and cofounder of the Social Progressive Imperative. A UK native and graduate of Oxford University, Green has worked in aid and development for the British government and taught economics at Warsaw University.

Author Kelly Kagamas Tomkies is a writer and editor with nearly 20 years of experience. Her published works include books and articles, as well as educational content for textbooks and publishers. She lives in Columbus, Ohio, with her husband, Kevin, and her son, Duncan, two dogs, a cat, and an African clawed frog.